ON HONEST

honesty is a th[...]
petals facing u[...]
begging to hang[...]

truth is an elastic nettle
stretching beyond
this coffee clutch of you and me

honesty doesn't have a clue
it meanders down pain
riddled roads telling it like it is

truth is reverent
sure it will live forever
like steam evaporating

honesty is transparent
illuminating the mom and dad
sideshow parenting is

truth is creative
conjuring flowers from spilt milk
sculpting survival from booze cans

honesty is punitive
unyielding ice sculptures
who refuse to melt

before I am honest
I want to witness
the beauty of a lie

MAPS

Maps are orders marching men to old places already seen.
Maps conjure memories of spoil, of plunder and innocence.
Maps are journeys to illusions no one has learned from.
Maps are critical revisits, visions of never before seen repeats.
Maps direct intentions, call attention and expose previous being.
Maps scatter reflection and delude wellbeing.
Maps flatten surfaces, time, distance, even height,
reduce critical illusions to trails of ink and colour.
Maps are pretentious,
arrogantly purporting to know where everything is,
pretending power where none is.
Maps are finite.
Maps are always old.
Maps never lead to uncharted places.
Maps flip our attention from being to place,
from metaphysical time, to streets, roads and clocks.
Maps cheat our prospective response to depth.

CLEAR WATER

only through clear water can we see wolf etchings carved on walls
my eyes obscured by old tears blind, I tip my face, a tear drop slips
slides into the river; it rolls past looking grateful to be going home

IT WAS

It was the laughter
maybe the stories
or the compliments
possibly the flirtation

It was the conversation
the moments of disclosure
traveling to understanding
the elevated blood levels

It was your face on a video
your voice sure and steady
lyrical wire-threaded smooth
and so gentle as a breeze

No, it was the storm
thunder bellowing
lightning covered sky
roads drowning sense

It was the chill of the night
or was it seeing your face
hurrying for the next note
the explosion of aliveness

ON HOPS

Before the moment the blood-red petals dripped from this branch,
this flower bloomed bright and the sweet morning dew dripped from
the petal's edges just as the sun kissed the rose and a yellow and black
jacketed bumble bee thrust its stinger into the centre of the flower
sparking the birth of a hip rich with nourishment.

Before the moment this hip reached maturity, the rain fell
pell-mell onto bald mountains unable to hold the wet
the soil dried, the rose bent under the pain of dehydration
shrivelled in the sun's cruel glare the hip failed to mature
failed to swell; we grew thirsty, so thirsty we settled for hops.

BLUE   JAY'S   GRASS   DANCE

grass people swing and sway
wind's breath waltz singing
whistling between green stalks

blue jay hip hops and tangos
some men swallow the sound
let it float across their throats

uttered this man song—flirts
textured voices layered sounds
the purple-gold song slides
between the ordinariness of talk

this grass-dance-blue-jay-song
wakes up spring in the blood
calls west wind's lust breath being

this is procreation's ceremony
of lust-love-blue-jay-grass-dance
the song is older than humans

between plain words and vocables
blue jay's dance spills onto the news
runners want to bring you up to date on

SNAKES

Gold diamond-backed snakes
slither between blades of grass
the green slivers cuddle him

                              Snakes await innocent prey
                              steal movement from the earth
                              and slide across the savannah

Snakes inspire ridiculous doubt
inspire caution, forcing research
by children who understand value

                                      The savannah ignites
                                        eliminates the grass
                                        squeezes children

The burning savannah
threatens snakes' habitat
rain squelches fire

                                      The snakes multiply
                                      wander into wasteland
                                      mouths slack, open, gold

Snake enters the children
procreates whirls of doubt
The whirls machinate

                                  twist into tornadoes of fear
                                  Fears paralyze their bodies
                                  the snakes' doubt lies quiet

Still for a while, the snakes
awaken during their days
of decision, drive them off path

EARTH QUILTS

In this blackened room
wanting windows
my body sweats
compressed by quilts

Each square originates
in some man's suit
Being sandwiched between
dreary beiges and browns
denies my body weightless
                              dreams

The room swells
dark fills it up
blocks feelings
warm pictures die
transforming my room
into a chamber of unreality
designed to opaque dreams

VIRGINS

Thighs pulled closed
by kitchen drudgery
laced shut by parrots
mimicking
      Whore
           Whore
                Whore
Constructing prisons
of bold black type
reading
      Sanctity
           Piety
                Decency
White

      Cold

              Pure

                    Still

dead

HELEN

      I felt La Pas's night
      press upon her body
      dangerous and cold
      Heard the car's hum
      murmuring threats
      cold steel rolling up
      its fire aiming at her
      The engine cuts out
      footsteps crunch gravel
      Saw drunken mad breath
      watched it sear her body
      hands claw at the cloth
      struggling to protect
      the fists unimpeded
      Hot rods tear her flesh
      her birthing place
      Bones crunch broken
      I repeat her name
          Helen…

          Helen…

                            going down
to stone to pavement
Helen, bleeding

          bleeding

                            going down

NIGHT COMES SOMETIMES

— bruised and sorry
Dark swallows light in bits and pieces
Unwilling, Dark hesitates
dances along the edge of light
rolls back and forth before day
As though
as though it knew beforehand
Dark was a cover
a harbour of protection
for those whose actions in the day
cannot be forgiven
As though
as though Dark thought somehow seeing was the thing
that was unforgivable
As though
as though somehow the doing under thick quilts
of black forgave
while in daylight
in daylight the sight of the doing rendered it horrific
As though
as though it knew
the night's gulping blackness would be blamed
would be made the hated thing
As though
as though she knew deed and doer would come back to
life
unscathed
and return to innocent black
in silence
free
free to reconvene the horror, the act committed not to
Dark
As though
as though night knew its very blackness was the judged
thing
its innocence stolen
stripped of her dreamscape
bruised under a foreign vision
beat up and sorrowed
she retreats
bent under its weight

BREATH SLIPS

breath slips across vocal cords
pearls of truth wriggle inside lies
inside the cords' folds they hum
collide with bravado masking hurt

a tug of war ensues
breath wheezes
        labours
flails at the air
plugs holes in spaces
                of emptiness
unhooks the chains of pearls
                            captured in the layers

breath pushes
        strains
forces voice to open
releases toxins, ooze
out thick and sluggish

    b   r   e   a   t   h
sweet air
    b   r   e   a   t   h
pearls of wind
stones of hope

WEST WIND

West wind's grass dance
drums a steady beat
not dulled by repetition

East wind pulls up belief
re-searches grass world
nurtures winded promise

Grass blades succumb to north wind
Trees surrender, sap stilled by cold
unabashed by winter's advance

South wind, exalted, hurries
to pull water, small miracles
arising out of dreaming rivers

SALMON DANCE
For Lawrence

I

There are no mountains to backdrop or reference where I am
Heat is curdling the food inside my belly
I squint under the glare of Visalia's brutal summer sun

Karen sits stoutly in a chair; the laughter textures her voice
"Here he comes," like it's some shared secret—I look
through the speckled light of walnut trees, there is this smile
his voice saying "hay-ay, Karen"

Cheam's winds whirl
west wind collides with Cheam's breath
They yarn themselves together
braiding my desire to the
dance going on inside
They play with my heart
sing salmon songs of promise
I float from the top of Se'ealth's mountains to this valley
of sage
of dust
of sun
To some other place of heat
of promise
of whirlwind romance

I know why them people call it falling in love

II

The kitchen is full of grown women
They wonder about their mom
complain about their dad
I ache

Karen's blood relatives form a clutch
my dad pretends he's not
Art scowls accepting responsibility for burying the mother of
his children
grimly determined to do the right thing
My mother pretends she's ok
She's not
She wonders what she did, what she didn't do

to prevent this moment with its terrible sharp edges
from becoming reality

My younger sister grieves not knowing our sister as an adult
Karen left when she was a child — you were so lucky she cries
you got to know her as an adult
you were always so lucky — so privileged
Does she know how unlucky I feel?
How much bigger such luck makes the loss

I stare at Karen, my mind spitting between thoughts

We fit
didn't we just fit?
Our likes and dislikes dovetailed
We fit, why couldn't you see that
feel that our spirits, our hearts, our minds
just fit so neatly

I have to leave this room of bustling busyness
of incomprehensible and unmanageable hurt
The porch looks good

I didn't see you arrive
so the "hay-ay" catches me off guard
My smile escapes despite the sharp shards of glass
paining my face
"Do I get a hug?" the additional vowels excite
I do
I do so need to be held

III
Los Angeles city centre is deserted

    Riots they say
Rodney King
a video
a court case and a declaration of innocence
sparked this ghost-town-like-LA-aftermath

I wander
try to think about you
try to call
try to persuade myself you have not gone and married again
I sprinkle tobacco all over the emptied sidewalks of LA streets
spill prayers
whisper quiet words of hope onto the hopelessness downtown
LA's stones
must now feel

When all else fails a couple of beers will drop the defences…

"Hay-ay, Lee, good to hear your voice"
South wind's breath trails through the sound his words make

Can I visit you sometime?

Sure, you know you're always welcome
anytime

I never asked who else would be there to greet me

North wind's breath bites into my courage
fills me with grim determination
I move
plan
execute the plan
I am on my computer
constructing letters
on the phone sharing my life
telling everyday stories about me
painting images of my personal mundane
receiving paragraphs with love…ending the page
hearing "love ya" over the phone like it was so understood
such a given

I am on the plane
flying across this island's expanse
in the airport
on your couch

lying on your chest

"I'm cold"
"That's because—little girl—you should be in bed,
under the covers"
(In your arms I tell myself
not struggling with the ache in mine)

I am afraid I will not ever want to leave

IV

I am home
snow quiet muffles the ache for you
West wind brings fresh storms
whirling howls of yearning breath
mountains of excitement
freezing rain
high winds
and finally spring punches a hole in the icy air
The plane rises
it lands
I move to greet you
you tap your lips
we kiss

"What do you want to do? It's up to you"
I thought I was up to my life
thought I could make decisions
willfully
These words ring oddly foreign in my ear
I like the sound of them, but find it difficult
to rise to the level the love of my life has established

The week burns holes in time
races to a close

Wait,
one more minute
one more second
one more touch
look
smile
kiss
one more…

WHERE IS THAT ODD YELLOW DANDELION-LOOKING FLOWER

Where is that odd wild yellow dandelion-looking flower leaning into the sun like it is trying to escape being swallowed by all that green salal, the heavy sun-purpled black huckleberries or the black brambles that explode with the kind of sweet flavour that wakes up every taste bud in your mouth?

I want to feel the smooth hard green surface of salal, immerse my eyes in the near ovoid shape of their leaves so tough, so shiny, so stubbornly peopling clear-cut mountainsides after the first spring rain.

I want to be that slender single blade of grass peeping from between crushed stone and lime-cemented sidewalks, unmindful that the whole city is covered with concrete, uncaring that lawn grass should not have to squeeze up through the sidewalk under people's well-heeled feet.

I want to know that fronds of cedar waving hello to old songs still hear me and understand me when I talk sparrow-talk to them. I want to rest assured they can translate our old agreements to this bird-talk-raggedy language with all its confused origins and sound that scrapes at the skin. I want to know that this sharp-edged language doesn't tear the scales off deep-sea salmon. I don't want to feel the bite of words against my yielding flesh.

When I speak to men I want the words to roll out easy and be received with the same grace my offering was made. I want these words to fill the basket of space between us and not open up wounds. I want words to wrap the listener in future, inspire him with hope and not arouse suspicion.

I want to know that the rage men feel is diminishing, that the permission they cradle in their souls to rape, to plunder, to kill is dying as I speak. I want to remember a world in which women were honoured, cherished and loved.

No more fires burning children, no more men fondling girls, no more beatings, no more bombings, no more push-me-pull-me power games that shame.

I want to hear the hushed quiet just before the hum of the quake the animals hear from some deep old memory handed to me when all life spoke the same language and agreed upon the simple things that had nothing to do with lining up, raising your hands to speak or stepping aside to pass.

I want to roll down the hill, express that roll in words so alive they inspire others to hike to the summit of my mountains and never want to cut another valley in two and fill it with dynamited hillsides someone used to straighten out a highway. I never want to see another highway built to extract the trees they could not get out the first time.

I hunger for a world where pain is a punctuation mark, not a steady heartbeat rhythm's dance on the soft side of the body, humming terrifying melodies, tuneless lyrics, to weary ears. I hunger for a world free of utilitarian nonsense that promotes exploiting people's desire for objects they don't need.

I want to enjoy gifts, the romance, the seduction, the oneness, the joy, the sorrow, the losses, the gains, the very dynamic that life presents in some easygoing kind of fulfilling way, the promise that being human was handed.

I want to live before I die.
— cj

I DANCE

I dance flute in hand
push sound through
hollowed out wood

I slow dance
let flute
define time

I dance on the edge
this old ceremony
carries me home

ON BEING A HERO

I'm taking this story
getting inside it
turning it inside out
so that I am the hero

ON THE 25ᵀᴴ ANNIVERSARY OF MARTIN LUTHER KING'S DEATH

I.   Pre-1960 Baby-talk

Birmingham has a ring
Ta'ah rolls it out slow
ending with an easy hum
The wood floors peel back
echo the name she makes
reshape it almost a song
Wind whistles through cracks
the shiplap accompanies
the floor, chanting
Birmingham, Birmingham

The black box is new
it visions story, black,
white, shades of grey
Far away people enter
the space of a table
that squats over pine
planks unfinished help
us to chant Birmingham,
Birmingham

A white man plays with it
images of children emerge
a moving photo drama
we still, still seated, stare
"They are black" from Ta'ah
like a reverent question
"From Africa," momma says
saying the A like it was holy
How do they know I say?
Still and silent, they nod

I don't get it.

The box with its moving kids
roars an unrecognizable sound
"Why are dey talking about
diss purse momma" Shsh
It chops the air, crisp, sandy
short. "Wa'atch" Ta'ah
intervenes on my behalf

I do.

The hollering elevates
the voices have a lilt
it gathers speed
increases volume
advances toward the children
words stretch themselves
beyond my familiar
but I know what they say

How do I know?

The breath in the room stops
the images in the box hold it
I watch the women watching
not the box, but the children
Birmingham black children
move backward, then forward
so together, so in unison
Uniformed men move then slow
they threaten their sashay
the children advance as though
they could threaten the uniforms
I cringe, "Disperse, go home"
the beings slow their movement
the children sway not toward home
but forward into the fray

The tension in this room thickens
something is going to happen here

The swaying short black people
take on a murmur, the men swing
sticks connect, a small girl screams
darts behind the line of bigger
children, the sound becomes words
"I ain't a scared a your jail
cuz I want ma freedom"
The swaying menaces
a crazy dance of defiance
We all rise to our feet, salute
Ta'ah and momma weep
their fists clenched

They remember something
I need to know, the sticks
the sticks hit their marks
children lurch into the swing
I cringe, scream in silence
N   O   O   O   O   O
The song swells, a tide
of children, singing, dancing
defiant falling, bodies bleeding
My momma sings the song
tears punctuate "ainta scared a
your jail," Ta'ah her poor
broken Inklish fights to sing
the song of justice from falling
bodies of children, "ainta shcaret
uff yer chail"—Are they crazy
do they expect me to be this black
this defiant, so willing to bleed
for a thing called freedom, shaking
someone has to tell me something

The newsman horrified
shouts, his camera struck
he falls, the box blackens
then light, someone seated
says "And that's the news
from Birmingham, Alabama"
My mother lunges at him

shuts him up mid-sentence
talking about the weather

My mother scares me
she shuts white men up
Ta'ah's body stills
"Remember, these people
have no shame" it fills
every corner, sucks up air
I am trying to breathe
I opt to swallow it

II.   Post-Martin Mother-talk

Martin has a dream
        me too
I dream of salmon runs
so thick no one hungers
cedars so old no one
is homeless, I dream swans
so loving no one murders
I dream barracudas sharking
mangling emotional insanity
crippling narrowed vision
bore holes in meanness
I dream rats perish
clean air peoples sky
sun blankets children

I dream Palestine to life
Bantustans into graves
Soweto back to language
a shared and precious thing
The world becomes slow
easy, in my dream
deep breath
soft breath
No sucking wind and shaking
no shallow panic, no breath
forced past tight vocal cords
no "stop   stop   please don't
please   my child   my baby
stop   please   stop   please"
Martin floats on the wind

riding an old cayuse,
Slahoot, Crazy Horse, Pappy
even Seattle calls out
"I ainta scare a your jail
cuz I want ma freedom"
Martin carries Sojourner's Truth
her laughing—him just being
both singing we shall overcome
Martin's dream breathes easy
where the red man, the white man
the yellow man and the black man
can live in peace, my pappy adds
And love the land, love the land

III.   1990 Oka-talk
I want peace
freedom from war
freedom from strife
freedom from conditions
which annoy the mind

IV.   2000 millennium Gramma-talk
Scraps of childhood memory
placed in a circle around me
There is Ta'ah, revering shame
momma shutting up white men
shut up for mouthing nigger
me shaking freedom into my belly
dreaming black dreams of peace
free air space, love, maybe joy
some easy kind of breathing

This dream is a bridge
inviting others to its arc
share this space
stand on it
string your dreams
make the arc swell
make the number
touch the sky

On this bridge
 across turtle's back
  free spirits still dance

FLUTES FAN FIRE SONGS

Flutes fan our fire song's flames
the sound embroiders burning coals
firelicks of light easing the burden
carried by women
Inside these firelicks pathfinders warble
flutes playing some imagined sound of grace
whose notes ring out impossibly delicate
The sound speaks of a fire-edged pillow
softening the landing
as each segment of this long journey ends

MY DREAMS STRETCH THIN
Music by Columpa C. Bobb
Outfront, CBC Radio
January 14, 2002

Begin with song (hum) slow fade and allow the music/
song to drift through the words, subdued

I carry bones
raven picked clean
Shards of my past
preserved in an apron
seashell decorated
I hold them close
they rattle in a particular way
making music between stories
that once opened my mouth

I make music from bones
sing shake-dance songs
chase out words used to silence
My bones insist I talk back

The stones inside
rivers and waterfalls
echo story the way
my bones echo song

      Subdued hum to full vocables, then fade

I lie across my grandpa's shoulders
He carved canoes and wove stories,
raven, push, jump and laugh stories,
dropping images of sea serpent,
raven and wolf into my consciousness

These characters hitched themselves
drop by drop to my innocence

I played with their sound, pappy's
rolled down to me slow and easy,
spinning a web of intimacy

From the stories a river

fluid and deep met sea
Raven secured me
myths, crafted dreams
linked them to memory

                Music gains volume, then fades

I scribbled stories, hope
promised these tracks
etched on the edge
of sacred cedar matured
and a book was born

Sometimes raven twists my words,
they fall at odd angles keypunching
nonsense words across my brain
in a jazzy kind of rhythm
These words ping pong
between raven's shrieking
back-up notes and jazzy tunes
under your bundle of noise,
drowning the symphony stories

Raven's jazzy drum forms
a marching band, the sticks
ricochet against old bones
I hear your words,
feel them enter my bones
They seize my elasticity
stretch it, it snaps
My clarity tenses
becomes wire
cuts my insides
binds me to a whirl
of unfamiliar being

At first your bone songs sang
open-throated songs of sweetness,
echoing the cadence of grandpa's
voice as he pulled me to his
shoulders and cradled
my frail and trusting body
My womb stretched, extended soft satin
invitations calling you to enter my world

I held my apron wide open, collected words
I braided fragility to your promises
All jazzed up and shiny it inspired
the raven in my soul, picked my way
across the stones on the path you cut
careful not to spill anything

My womb leaks desire
plays music
an old salmon dance

                Music rises

I did a two-step country dance across rocks
shuffle, rattle and shake, click, click, click

                Music snaps out

I pretend your bones are the same as mine

                Music rises, fades

I float along your concepts of romance
Dance through words, wrap my affection
around the notions you proffered
on my bones
Your songs scratch my desire
try to drown my first love
I dropped my words

I scribbled my dreams
rebirthed by grandpa's old story
hid my raven sketches from view

It was not enough for you
One night when the wind chilled
the fire in your bones
you discovered my word etchings

Your words became blows
I sat helpless while your arms
hammered at my body,
pummeled my mind into a bizarre
puddle of defeat

Your fear is a being
He gathers together memory,
conjures extraordinary failure
to engage my affection
Your fear cannot cherish

Fear is a tormenter
Hiding my being from me
he lies to my spirit,
persuades my body
it is weak, vulnerable

Fear is seductive
soft-voiced, rhythmic
He owns an iron trap
whose memory betrays

Fear is alive
He erases victories,
eradicates possibility,
short changes my river words

Fear diverts my journey

Fear is a valve
opening cells to viral incursions
Fear instructs my cells to give
give up, give a leg
up to this intrusive viral hate
I treat my memory as though
it were the invader
Boost your hate from cell to cell
until I became your host

My story bundles scatter on the floor
The noise of your memory frees you
to reconvene horror upon my body
It stopped my mind
from remembering grandpa,
my skip jump raven stories,
my sea serpent and wolf
My bruised body cannot recall
the assurance of grandpa's shoulders

Your nightmare behaves as though
somehow my vision of myself
as a writer was unforgivable
As though the destruction of my writing
could quiet the din going on in your mind
As though my desire to imagine
could be made the hated thing

As though thick quilts of nightmares
gave you permission
to render my life horrific
As though you really could
strip me of my dreamscape
As though my beaten body
could sorrow so deeply
I would retreat forever,
bent under the weight of grief
As though your fists could divorce me
from my apron of bone words

                Music/song rises, fades

Bones talk at night
under stars who hum sweet songs to dark
Bones insist on dreaming-speaking
My night hesitates to hear these bones
Night dances along the edge of light,
rolls back and forth
as though it knew beforehand the words,
as though driving your violence were a cover,
a harbour of protection forgiving your fists

My bones speak to my dreams,
repeat grandpa's stories
His warm currents of meaning
sing an old stomp-dance blues tune
to my battered flesh
reminding me of my words

Awakened by my bones,
I remember Salish women
never eat second-hand meat
I pick up each bone word
from my puddle of fear,

examine each one
They murmur their joy at my return
I fall in love with the sound they make

I caress each bone,
full of paragraphs of belief
they sing songs
from a pool of ancient meaning
The songs punch through your hate

My fragility is agile,
unwilling to accept defeat
it leaps from tender to tensile
swallows your madness
the sea of seduction
my fear has become split
In the divide
I open myself to paragraphs
of forever words I own

My dreams stretch thin
My fear rages, but my night
cannot forgive me
My original songs will not lay quiet
My stories will not accept defeat

Inside these stories lies my courage
I hide them in the soft folds
between the layers of fear you inspired
and the courage I denied
The sound of my courage is willful,
it hothouses a compelling activism
I am compelled to share

                    Music/song rises

The sound of my courage is loud
The volume of its determined staccato
stabs at my fear

In my dark night of communion
I pick up my bundle of bones
my words become swords

These swords, polished by belief,
flash their bright edges

I am deaf to this fear of you
I shake the remnants from my apron
I spray golden hues of gentle light
across my fragile moments,
weave a steely yarn of consciousness
into the fabric of my song,
hitch it to my being, divorce
those who cannot cherish the sound
my bone words make

I am not who I claimed to be
I believed I belonged to you
like some old moccasin
some piece of jewelry
some bone crashing
about in the bundles you held

I decline to be your plaything
I embrace my stories
retrieve their meaning

I feel them re-enter my bones
These bones that are stones
cradle whole lives,
become a kaleidoscope
of Suquamish story

I sing these stories to blank white pages
pen bone word songs of unfettered being

                Music ends the piece

You did not come to my table empty-handed,
inside your body were your own bone songs
Your bundles were loaded with stones full of acid rage,
each inseparable water drop sound from your voice
fell into my belly to form a fragile lake of torment,
taunting my fragility

Scratching at my desire,
burning my need to create story

I could not stop dreaming

My hope falters
My voice shrinks
My voice instructs me
in the direction of defeat

Your nightmare behaved as though
my vision of writing was unforgivable

As though the destruction of my writing
could quiet the din going on in your mind
As though my desire to imagine story
could be made the hated thing

FALSE FACE

Truth frightens
Fear seduces
Paintings stretch
False face teaches
us to stand on guard

OKA

On June 23rd Elijah whispered no
killing the accord, and for 18 days
we rejoiced
Until the guns went off at Oka,
we thought we really could
                                        just say no

TORONTO RIVERS

Toronto rivers babbled

catapulted over cliffs

tossed themselves down hills

dragging dirt, pebble and stone

carving a space

clearing a channel

getting ready for another fish run

Now the lonely waters mumble

barely audible from inside culverts:

free me,

                free me,

                                free me...

How much progress is in that?

SILENT HILLS

cry to the wind
stripped naked
they stand facing the sun
helpless to stop the D-9 cats
from gouging life from them
Tomorrow the drills will come
digging mineshafts to ease extraction
even the sweet green hair covering
my Ta'ah's grave burns yellow
in the shadeless Shuswap sun
    burnt wood
    dead grass
    toxic rivers
Dried earth-dust follows wind
in search of a safe new home
There isn't one, the caretakers
have all nipped into the pub for a wet
  When they're not tippin'
   back the amber
  they're sleeping it off

THIS CIRCLE

is a wheel
encased in glass
It cracks
like crabs

We
    s
       c
              a
                        m
                                p
                                      e
                                            r

to freedom

RAVEN   CAWS
cackles   hallo   from   the   tips
of   a   not   so   blue   spruce
straggling   to   stay   upright
Needles   disease   reddened
skin   cracked   and   dry
in   its   decadent   agitation
its   branches   want   to   fall

Raven   shrieks   terrified
She   perches   uneasy
on   the   cracking   tips

Cedars   below
diminished   by   logging
deliver   new   babies
hum   a   death   song
to   the   clear   cut
Raven   doesn't   speak
to   cedar   anymore

MINNOWS

Inside the maze of sea grass
sockeye minnows focus
on barracudas
sending sharks
into feeding frenzies
        Quantities of blood
        flood their view
cloud minnow consciousness
Shark-death fractures their good sense
obscures the nature of their yearning

FILLETS

Filleted images
scraped free of dimension
elude me
The fillets float just out of reach
the slowest hand movement
cannot retrieve them
cannot clutch the dream slices
The wedges dance and haunt
slip-slide
taunt
My skinny scraped images sigh
and smile at me

9 1 1

In a mere quatrain of poetic time
the mere slice of a stanza
two collapsing towers bent the
imagination of the world
away from peace
Enticed electro-hyped
re-runs of leaping bodies
parts uncovered
a hand almost unrecognizable
a torso—too small to want or resist war
twists human eyes
riveted to massacre
The child bleeds revenge into the souls
of his family
and binds me
to a new aggressive dynamic

PLAY WITH LANGUAGE

I pull at strings connected to this alphabet
I so want to win, let me win just this once
Can't believe I will gamble on an alpha
anything

30-SECOND LOVE POEM

Murdoch Burnett's Gaelic upper body
plunges into my air space
reddened brown waves of hair
comically handsome white face

Says he will introduce me
"Is there anything special
you want me to say about you?"
Now there's a loaded pair of dice

He hands me his poem
after four lines and five minutes
I fall in love
                for about thirty seconds

ROSE PETALS

rose petals drift
land on the linen
vase transforms
becomes a sentry
guarding remains

OUR DARK PALLET

Shafts of light split
fray visibility
sprinkle thin ribbons
of light on taut skin
stretched cheekbones

Hair loosens
tangles
untangles
Veins open
scrape away
he fabric spidered
across our dark pallet

WOOD

wood gives
under the urging of blades
cut by chainsaw blades, the cutting
diminishes the lightness of its being
earth's other children have a memory
this memory threatens serenity
wood chips fly
carving
chases flights
too many instructions
carve holes in children's hearts
I delete them, fill myself with reams of nonsense

PARADIMES

Dangling confusion
presses up against walls
of my bent box

Paradimes
scrape its carved
fragility, threatening
the box's bent shape

Disempowered intellectuals
seek social parallels
ignore the paradigm
implied by bent box

TORONTO WOLF

The wolf tracks still linger
imprinting Toronto's story
under paved trails, memories
cuss-loaded and crass
hover above streets
Leaves flip and fly
trying to articulate
in ovoid language
wolf's aspirations

The shapes lighten our step
We trip over wolves' words
decaying between the cracks
exposing teeth guarded by lips
who knew the steppers' swollen
feet belong to manufactured
dead eyes open only to prices
Dead orbs emerge from brains
that never question production
or the real price of anything

The leaves land quiet, careful
not to disturb the tracks

JAGGED EDGED STONES

In the moment it was difficult to appreciate
stones covering my path
    so I didn't
    I worked at living
I laughed and sang at just about everything
gathering bits and pieces of knowing from
whatever corner of the earth would give it to me
I tucked this knowing in old tattered shirts
    torn jeans
    cheap shoes
I scraped my knees on more than one stone as I
knelt to earth
    to wind
    to rain
Tattered and fatigued, I kept going not stopping
to look at the trail,
afraid to see the sharpness and doubt the journey
was worth it
I hopped, stepped and jumped from stone to
stone, stole smiles
    from the light
    grabbed courage
I finally cast a backward glance; I can still see
those old stones
sharp, in between them is all this colour, shafts
purpling the trail
gold, scarlet-yellow spikes lighting me up and me
shuffling
    In retrospect
    I loved the ride

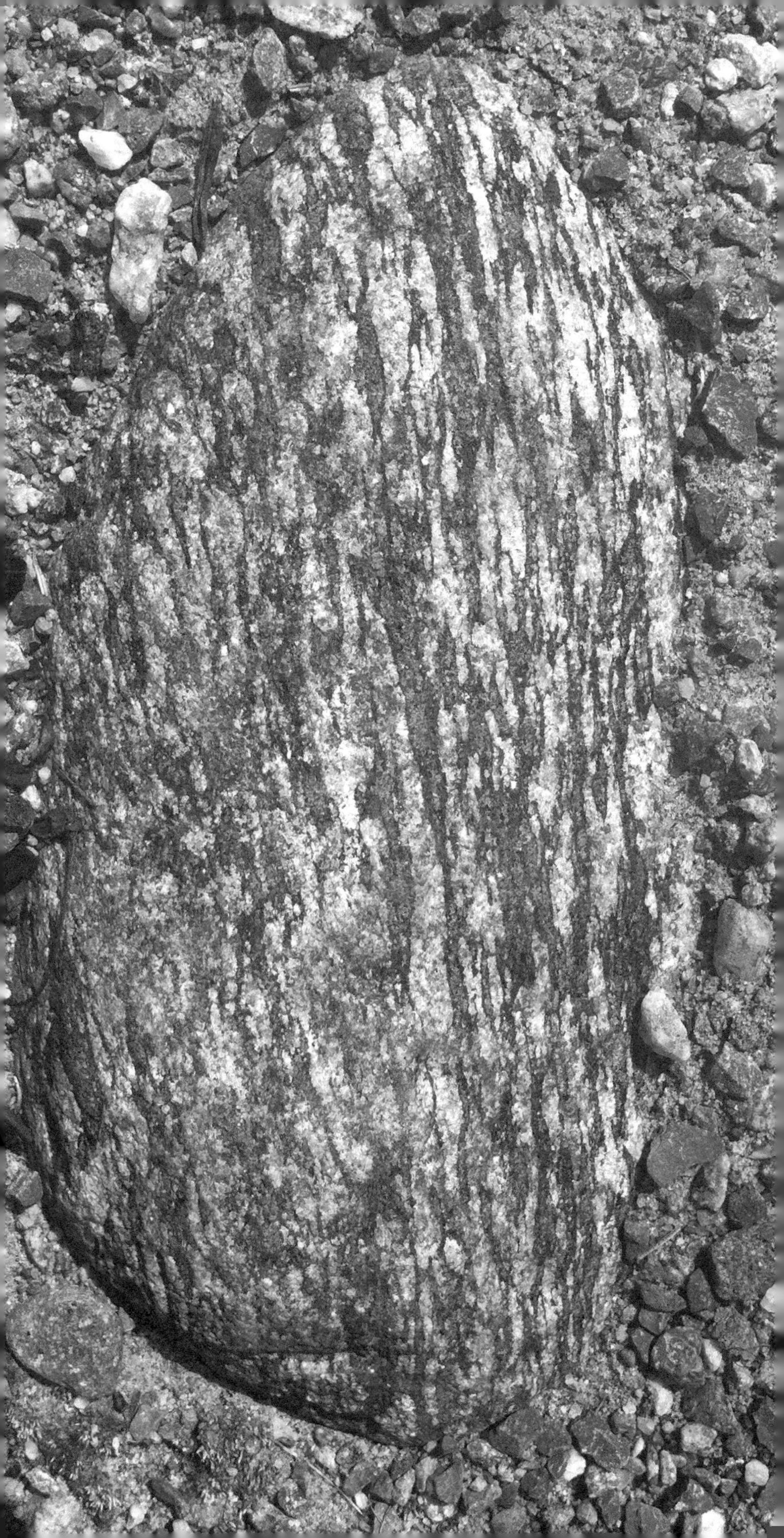

DECEMBER 6TH

Sharp sounds cut joy into pieces as the lead
pierces your bodies
Bodies explode, blood slips from the holes
desecrating your song
My mother's skin cringes; she holds her
breath, wrestles shock
her breath, sticks, captures the air, freezes,
suspending time

Wails override the space these youth graced
      Thin arms grab one last moment
      desperate to halt the flood of
      blood

The television details your departure
the commentator lists your names
Your names fight for life, for memory
for realization, I glue them to my mind

The earth is offended as blood fills the spaces
between yesterday and today — December 6th
it rolls off the tongue so normal on this day

My mind is a tornado
whirling around what was murdered
complacency   apathy   complicity
I can't stop listing the death here
the children you might have had
your life as engineers, fighting angles
lines, formulas, the everydayness of you
the giggles, the gossip from cafeterias
classrooms
dormitories
your responses to traffic
to weather

to touch
all dead
      The earth wants to howl
      to whip wind, to object
      this is not about a man
This is about blood exploding
the murder of the sacred
the bludgeoning of future

All life is sacred
my mother keeps repeating
as daughters' bodies spasm
bleeding fragments of life
curled in fetal position
I cringe "All life is sacred"
I murmur from my chair
My breath wraps around images
tries to make sense of a world
that created this sensibility
stealing your life too soon

CANADA IS A LABYRINTH

1. An intricate [having many complexly arranged elements—soluble or comprehensible only with painstaking effort] structure [a complex entity, the constitution, organization of such an entity], passages [act or process of passing; the right to pass; a corridor for passing]
2. Something highly intricate [complex], in composition [putting parts together to make a whole] or construction [to form by assembling parts]
3. A group of communicating [imparting news, transmitting information, passing on an infection, illness, intimacy, understanding, just about anything] anatomical [of or relating to the science of animal, plant or bodily structures] cavities [a hollow within a solid body, a decayed part of a tooth]
4. The internal ear, comprising the semicircular canals, vestibule and the cochlea

From Middle English, from Greek, from Latin, probably akin to Greek, probably borrowed from Caria [I don't know this place]

Canada is a labyrinth
full of dark passages
gatekeepers block entry
I enter cautiously
sneak past guards
My Latin is weary
so connected to priests who thrust
their sexuality into our child bodies
and drowned our sense of self
profaning my limited Latin

My Middle English remains foreign
not having any ancestral memory
before it modernized itself
I am rendered late in the speaking of it
I have no Greek Kin

The origins of Labyrinth
slides by my internal structures
In my simplicity, the complexity
of my arrangements becomes irrelevant
requiring no further comprehension
I leave the myth of understanding
to the imagination of listeners
Painstaking efforts will not assist
my passage through here

I am never sure if passage
limits my right to pass
speaks of a means to pass
or a simple corridor to pass

I hesitate
How can I speak to it?
I opt for a group
of communicating
anatomical cavities

My womanhood ejects
men waving weapons
forcing entry into passages
other than their own
The soft folds close
my mouth slurs
words of endearment
to the mouths of others
echoing rejection of assault
My ears close the corridors
to the sound of insult
underlying prohibition
of any one's right to pass

TALKING TO THE DIASPORA

Forced out
The spatial or geographic property of being scattered over
a range
a volume
an area
worldwide in distribution
+++++

On Turtle Island anyone who is not Indigenous
is part of some Diaspora
+++++

I wonder about language with its raw frayed fringes
    delicately trying to express spirit
as each word drips from lips to rest in blank spaces
    between us
Mangled by emptiness, the words are deflowered
When addressed this Diaspora
sometimes responds, debating,
educating, arguing, buying time,
stealing fifteen minutes from our space
this quarter hour so vital to our desire to regroup
    profanes our peace

I gather alphabetized concepts of Xa'al
    slice into its heart and open veins
I carve Xa'al's paragraphs onto trees, pulverized and flattened
under the flat-white surfaces, ancestral bones rattle
    play an old game of Lahal
    My sticks know these songs

From the summit of mountain ranges
words fall through the Diaspora's moral sky holes
In their descent they scrape meaning from cliffs
words blend with the chaotic rhythm of crushed rock
bind them to the plastic saran-wrapped food
perverted oil fuel Styrofoam-insulated buildings

It's a crazy kind of song
the mountain cliffs contort, the captains send infantry
Stripped naked, reshaped surfaces children can't play on
        each transformed object screams
        buy me, I will transform you
Base advertisements claim power can be yours
just buy this bobble, 99 cents, be the daughter

of an Ozzied Harriet caricature erasing blemishes

Under the bared skin of scarred mountains
stone is syringed, battered and extricated
dragged out by and lathed into new spears
to become bullets aimed at children
the relatives of others of the Diaspora
The captains conjure killing machines
erasing meadows and eradicating gullies
The eye line of progress becomes civilized
cheap labour's coinage—exchange power

Progress offends future
kills the monarch butterfly
wings flapping ineffectual
starves bees, melts ice

                                    Progress has no song
        Bell pops without resonance
        its smooth ring arrested
        The interrupted rhythm
        becomes ocean salt dreams
        waves cresting then perishing
        Progress's toxic froth
        bleeds red sunsets
        curls around old fires

chanting the rhythm of Tsleil Waututh drums

Words can break irascible barriers
        compress time
        measure being
        measure beats
        squeeze time

Words lodge in the tissue inside muscle and bone
brace the body for communion not always desired

I wonder about language
as humans close the space
between invitation, exclusion
the elephant in the room
where language is warm, fired
unmentioned, centred on entry
The captains are marauders
bellowing from the summit
riddling landscape with gouges
Mottled words riddle meaning
they betray expression
and demand inclusion

Xa'al slices the marauder's moments into thin wisps
exposing culpability, their bloodless decision making
Xa'al, energy, points to paragraphs of desecration
        These captains have heard our songs
        the bone songs compete with bellows
Everyone who dares to doubt progress is excluded

                              Progress has no melody

Incarcerated in bloodletting
metropolitan nightmares
        drown justice
        Hands out,
        dancers wave to sunrise
as the sun sets
It opens its own veins, fries ice
storms, trees pop and snap
decorating the world in destruction
        My ancestors halt breath
        mouth glottalized x's
        Machu Picchu to Iqaluit
voices circle the globe, earth moves
Progress thrives on children's blood
        No one copes

> **Progress is a corporate superstition**

Corporate myth inspires global toxicity
> Its mythology is omniscient

Sockeye, cedar, even raven prefer death
to challenging its legendary omnipresence
The surreal nightmare hounding earth
driving sockeye to scurry to outside edges
of sanity, scrambling for one last gasp at reason
failing, the poisoned water drives her to suicide
> This is not such an odd response

The suicide swim seems almost courageous
normal, as she arrives too early to procreate
she fails to subject her young to toxic life
> What would be the point?

Sockeye's heart cringes
cuts frantic spirals in open ocean playgrounds
baked too warm for her to know what time it is
It must have felt right, this suicide run upstream
> rapids pound her thin frame
> grey smoke explosions

send children to the altar of sockeye's suicide
> devouring feminine hope

Some bombed village crashes to the street
weapons cheer her on, clap, spit and bark
> bone fragments fly
> bleed rose on the pavement
> breath halts

A sharp rifle crack binds her to the empty womb of others
> pulling a last shout

from the grey smoke-filled Palestinian landscape

> **Desperate people don't make clean decisions**

Cobalt-hued polished steel shafts
> exterminate joy

intervene in the easy journey
> Breath rasps
> shreds
> swallows sanity

As though it were the monarch fighting to butterfly its way
> through a hurricane

while earth rushes herself to a new season
before the old one has been properly interred

                              Grey smoke is ruinous
               Ruins sit stable, still
               long after the red blood creeps
across them to seep between mortar crevices
               slips rose-hued under the rain
               of progress's cover up

                         Memory ruins only recent grandeur
               Memory is tricky
               it rests silent, ruins blood's slippage
               Was it like this before?
               Mad suicide plunges
               into the face of grey-smoked murder
               Memorial ruins piled upward to star heights
               bragging about progress
               as though poking holes in the earth's
               blue-sky shawl could be progress
I wonder about grandchildren removed from suicide
               a plan held hostage by corporate captains
               exploding lead, tailing toxins, leaching earth
pouring fire-stripped adulterated non-food into children

These maniacs fail my capacity to understand
Understand, understanding, standing under
What am I standing under?
Standing under this dome of avarice
Excusing bloodletting mystifies
          Even cedar weeps
Wind drafts uptake the words in the direction of sky holes
          Our mother throws torrents of rain
          hurricanes and tsunamis
          desperate to cover the hold
Monarch bodies drift up, twirl, fall and rise
drop again, cascade into a heap of millions
These millions speak mountains to those whose
bones lay dispirited beneath the blacktopped trails
their clear view of falling like the twin towers

As the earth is led to her own funeral
for those whose hearts beat quickly
          as they lust for gold
Will they remember my mother's dismembered body?
          Will they remember sockeye?
          Her bombed two-legged

clear-cut tree people, portals to financial cathedrals
erected on blood, of slaves, of stones, our stones

Will I be remembered as a decrepit flower?
unwilling to articulate the seed blooming assurance
a perennial cedar, cones minimizing annihilation?
Will my words dangle from empty raped mountains?
           laid to waste on dead seas
Or will they sing sweet from the skirt of winds
remembered songs of hope not realized?

      Being is fragile
      a slip of thread about to snap
      a scrap of memory fading
      an unprocessed thought
      an unrealized desire
      a mute expression
      a repressed emotive direction
      a silenced song
      a held breath, light, dusky
slow, thrifty flight of fancy to nowhere
A question without the punctuation mark
trailing into some voice constricted
locked inside a throat too dry to bellow

      Being is simple
      it answers death
      questions birth
      imagines connection
      authenticates activism
Being falls martyred into the lap of belief
      Being conjures myth
attracts fiction to truths direction
      Being masks false faces
Being is a split second lumbering slow march
      into our last hour of flight
challenging the glare of marauders
      Being dreams in sacred dark
      Being is and all
and so is in danger of slipping,
    slipping
        slipping
            slipping

Progress fears failure

Failure is a flower, the seed is knowledge
From conception all knowledge begins wilting
    at the green stem of its beginning
This flower is adored by those whose views
include green mountain vistas, olive branches
clear rivers charting a wet road to the sea
The flower's perfume is the scent of death
    just before her seed spawns birth

Grey obscures the glare of ozone-tampered sun
    of a melted Arctic shelf
    its ice fields crack,
trick society, careening upstream
sanity stretched beyond madness

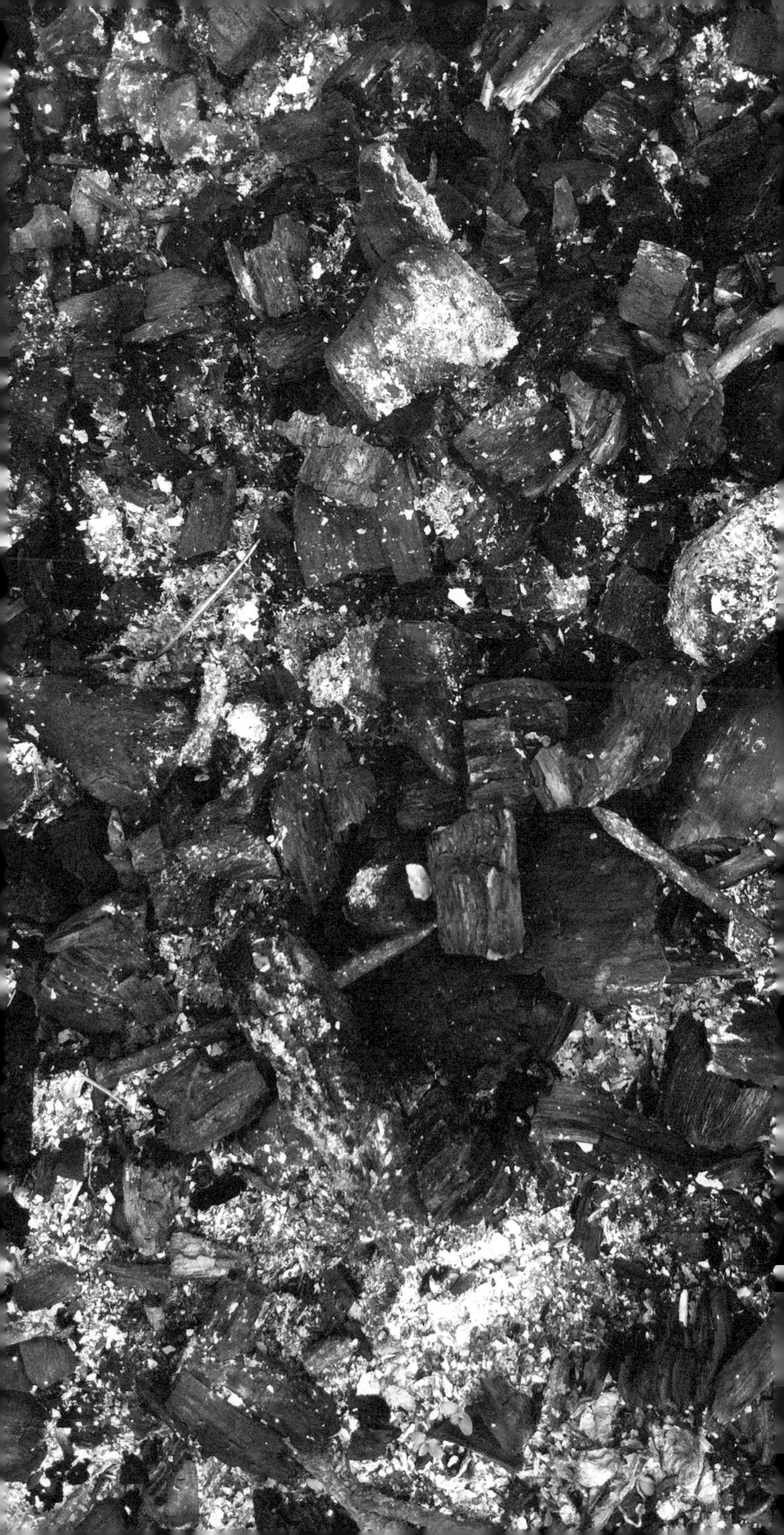

NIGHTSKIES

Night skies drift over Turtle Island
dropping dark mournful tones
waiting for sun to return to kiss the earth
to bathe her in soft frosted yellow light

Night skies fill the space between earth's
warm body and star nations' wondering world
Come night sky, come to me love the way I lay
paint warm black dreams onto my open skin

Night skies come to me bringing memories
of brown-skinned woman facing east
watching sun's rise over billowing sails
anticipating the ship's visitors, innocent

Come to me night skies, wrap me in black
loving midnight blue moon paled light
Whisper sweet words, soothe my aching body
warm my heart to my anticipating life

Night skies come holding breath, crunching
words of trapped souls stuck here in the pale
between earth's body and the edge of her breath
Trapped souls waiting for their last ride home

Night skies come sharing the breath of bodies
bodies bleeding, screaming of blood everywhere
These spirits recant stories of encounters of
the first kind. Hush night, let me rest, hush night

Bayonets glisten in my dark. Sharp cold
reflective light in the hands of men
whose spirits spent dip steel sticks into
fragile bodies of women come to greet them

Night sky come to me, come to love me
Wrap yourself around me, bring me to the place
where my heart can find the breath to speak
to the women whose blood still paints the soil

Night sky come to me, come love me that I might
lay tobacco out—face these women
hear them tell me the ceremony they need
to ask Star Nations to take them home

Night sky come to me, reach for breath's origin
Fill me with the voice I need to sing the song
that will show the star trail these women need
to make that long journey home—come sky

Night skies velvet touch dances across
in dreaming beauty, ceremony emerges
frees my spirit, settles the quandary
of the entrapped spirit women dancers

Night sky comes, grabs moonbeams
layers them between star nation and earth
Night whispers come home child—come home
leave this island with its blood, its cold and its death

Night skies return breathing dreams
of love, of life, of future, removing the
spiritual residue of blood, of death
awaken my body to sun, to wind, to song

SOME SONS

some sons are ravens, shapeshifting, transforming, flipping wings of feather at soft black dreams, transforming them into wrought-iron concepts that will cradle the journey from beginning to future on wingtips whose job it is to carry messages of moments sandwiched between the past, present and future, hoping those whose feet plant themselves firmly in the present will see the awesome film of colour that leads them to the space between worlds colliding.

some sons are wolves, jogging their vision between piss tracks demarcating territory, hauling hope in jaws loaded with sharp teeth whose eyes pierce holes in midnight's dream-space just above the territory they will never share with the world, but before they move to restrict access to their territory they invite communion with the crow riding their shoulder, letting her sneak a peek at the end of future's trail.

some sons are bears, medicating our world view from the same old, same old crazy pictures that dance in our heads, convincing us that all is as it should be until it has become an insane direction that we imagine is heaven and not simply the earth's children enjoying our life. this medicine rescues us from a wild kind of self-destruction, relocates us on a path where our beginning rests so easy we are hopeful.

some sons are frogs, legs squat on lotus leaves, croaking in unison, crying out to wolf, to raven, to bear, for the moment, investigating their stories, wondering about the journeys, examining transformation, finding a gauge from inside their creaky throats to evaluate the persuasive oratory of land animals so they decide to leap in unison.

UNTITLED

The light of my arc reaches the precipice,
trails itself to the end of earth's breath
These ends hook themselves to each shore
on this bridge of light across turtle's back
free spirits dance

GASSY JACK'S CLOCK

Gassy Jack's clock pumps out memories of displacement with each chug of steam. The urban renewal project's spin-off is homeless Indians. Every street houses memories of this process. It always has. Countless visitors and new arrivals take this tour. A hundred years of history is not easily packed into such walkabouts. How do you tell people about the intimate secrets a city hosts?

Not far from Gassy Jack's clock Khatsalanogh dug graves, grabbing sleep in bits, until he finally succumbed. He must have been lonely. It is comfortable and easy to forget him. He struggled to recover. They came for him and the women and children still left in his village. They loaded everyone on a barge and pushed it in the direction of the sea. After the sickness died, a sawmill squatted in his village for nearly a half century.

Just off shore from this city, the Komagata Maru sat, loaded with passengers destined for Vancouver. Detained. Do not debark. India would not take them back. They languished aboard the close quarters of the ship without water—starved and hungry. Parts of the left over ship languish in the museum—a hard iron-rusted reminder of this country's beginnings.

Unions formed to block non-white
participation in the labour market.
Laws were conjured based on this
desire. Because no one but white
men could form an organization
or lobby government, vote or influence
politicians, they came to dominate
everything and we went hungry.

The second narrows fell before anyone
got to travel on it. We did our duty
then, jumped in canoes and pulled
workmen out of the water, some dead,
some alive. I remember riding in the car
going up Keith Road hill. My little
sister and I glance at the concrete
and steel cutting an arc across a piece
of the skyline. We do this every time we
make this ride, to mark its progress.
It was fine, almost done, and magic.
Then her little voice full of awe says,
mommy, the bridge fell. We don't
believe her. We look. *It's gone. How
did it get gone? It was just there. It
fell.* There was once a village at one end
of the bridge. It died too, not as quickly
as the bridge, nor as painlessly as the
men on the bridge, but it is just as dead.

DIFFERENT VOCABLES

Some songs are lexically running vocables
escaping their grip on truth as they drop
from desperate lips uttering nonsense
escaping phrases like, *You have a son.*

I borrowed him from some star path
I crossed in a dream
and after I mopped his backside
a thousand times, did somersaults during hot
days when the sun attacked, bled his nose
and reddened his exposed back, I gave him to someone
who may never understand or love me.

Oxymoron describes a put together phrase
that makes no sense like *virgin timber*
but there is no way to express the
oxymoronic declaration: *I have a son.*

I heard his shrill cry
floated for an instant
before the baritone announced
"You have a son."
I search for this son they tell me I have
this search cost me endless new wardrobes
from unlikely boutiques with sexless names
like K-mart, Zellers or Wal-Mart.

I search around corners
in cupboards, under beds
the sticky texture of my web
of doubt envelopes my body
becomes tense, each failed attempt
to find him, makes me lose myself.

I hunt for his mind, his cooperation
his integration into some concept
of familial being, while I repeat
the same phrases: "eat, eat up,
eat, yummy, yum, eat…come here,
come, no, come here, come…up,
up, yes lift up, up, your arms, up,
up." I give up looking for him
and hunt for myself.

He starts school and I search
for myself in work, I fill out
forms, submit to interviews
The question: Is English
your second language
always accuses—I answer, Yes
right after baby talk.

I didn't get the job.

HOME FROM WORK

It's seven thirty
home from work
her bag drops
she slips off her coat
it falls
to the floor
as she sinks
into her only chair
the yellowing walls
blend into
the blank crevices
of her mind
forcing out the dreams
she woke up with
this morning

MY BINOCULARS

My binoculars peer
at the sins of others
through their tunneled
cylindrical peepholes
I hope it's the tunnels
distorting the images
of snake's and toad's
unforgiving warts

TORONTO STONES

Stones hold sound, forever locked voices

speaking through stone—grandfathers

stone sings of what could have been

Toronto's stones crushed under wheels

of cranes, dump trucks and bulldozers

Each pebble repeats songs of river death

gathered to murder the rivers with alacrity

Torontonians sashay along the pavement

under the crushed stone, voices scream

beg for release from the secrets of horror

REMEMBERING MAHMOUD 1976

Mahmoud's poems are beads of sweat
dripping from stressed and weathered foreheads
to fall near silent amid incessant Israeli bombs
to rise—blood—from between the bits of rubble
clutched by Palestinians chasing a livelihood
from a shrinking land base
They become desperate word flowers
blooming nonetheless from a land
occupied by settlers
chronically stealing the lives of children

It's December
        Toronto
Gaza is on fire
        again
another Wounded Knee
another massacre
no muskets this time
tanks, monster machines
bombs and missiles pummel the children
How brave is that?

-40 Celsius in Winnipeg
Palestinians and Indigenous children wave placards
Stop killing children in Palestine
Free Gaza
My tears freeze on my face
my daughter is there
just as she was there 35 years ago
chanting Free Palestindians
my frozen tears cut pain lines on my face

In between the rubble
Darwish's last words look at the world
say good-bye to Edward Said
peer past the camps, the bombs, the hypocrisy
stubborn
resistant
eternal
        There is no tomorrow in yesterday,
        so let us advance

I stare at a photo
a small boy cradles a pair of stones
gleaned from the rubble
I imagine him hearing
Darwish's ghostly words
these stones testify
this is his home
he clutches them
he looks set to advance
the stones are no longer simply rubble
they cradle a story
they cradle his memory
they cradle his hope
they cradle Darwish's last testament:
> *There is no tomorrow in yesterday,*
> *so let us advance*

In this boy's hands the stones transform
they are the story markers of his future
they are his beginning
beloved stones, last bits of a place called home
they become stones of conscience
they are his stones of pride
they will become his stones of belonging
they are the rocks of justice for all of us

His face is set
his eyes see past this rubble
they see forward to his return
forward to the restoration of his homeland
forward to the right of return
In his eyes I see Indigenous global tenacity
I touch the stones in the photo
caress his face
commit to building a bridge
an arc of light
under this wind of war
of dispossession
I want to build a pathway
and blow us all toward freedom and justice
I want the wind of freedom to echo
the resonance of Mahmoud's breath tracks

Let us pick up this stone of justice
build this bridge
that will lead us to the laughter of belonging
of being where we belong
of being who we are and always will be

This light shines back at me from his eyes
the light illuminates his stones
bound as these stones are to his resolve
to traverse across the abyss
between his refuge and the tanks
My commitment to Palestine floats
the light emanating from his eyes captures my heart
I whisper Palestine, Palestine—Free Palestine
Wounded Knee, no more Wounded Knees
I imagine him listening, hearing me
nearly smiling
just   before   he   throws   his   stones

THE LONG AND SHORT OF IT

My skin is smoked
so it is a little raw
My heart bleeds
solid songs of rage

BLIND JUSTICE

Ts'leil Waututh, Chaytoose, Snauq'w
the mountains rise behind my ancestors
and disappear in the sale of them
orchestrated by a department that seeks
their vanquishment—$25.00 becomes millions in the blink of an eye
    $25.00 becomes hunger in the next blink
becomes inadequate in the next blink
becomes the murder of cedar, sea vegetables, ouske,
whale and sockeye
as I struggle to mature without food
I am sorry too Mr. Harper

Sustained Violence
We could have recovered from smallpox
we had Xway-Xway
we had medicine
we had healing songs and dances
but they were banned

Violation
We could have recovered
we had friends
Christian friends
but they too were banned
My relations were banned from speaking,
    organizing, or fighting for land rights,
    fishing rights,
the right to sing and dance,
to raise our children,
to educate them
We could have included you in our ceremony
of facing ourselves
recovering ourselves
transforming ourselves
but our ceremonies were banned

Still, I am not tragic
not even in my addicted moments
a needle hanging from the vein of my creased arm
I was not tragic
even as I jump from a boat in a vain attempt to join my ancestors
I am not tragic

Even in my disconnection from song, from dance
I am not tragic
Even in seeing you as privileged
as an occupier of my homeland in my homeless state
Even as men abduct as I hitchhike along these new highways
to disappear along this lonely colonial road
I refuse to be tragic

My body has always understood justice
everyone eats and so we included you
there is no word for exclusion, so your whiteness is no threat

We have lived for 11,000 years on this coastline
this is not the first massive death we have endured
we girded up our loins
recovered and rebuilt

We are builders
we are singers
we are dancers
we are speakers
and we are still singing
We are dancing again
we are speaking in poetry
in story, in film

In the millennia that we have lived here there are constants
the tide will retreat and it will return
the fishes that are threatened will return
the people who died during those epidemics are returning
the plants, the trees, the animal world will recover
It may take another Tsunami of the sort that nearly killed us all
It may take earthquakes and storms
but the earth, the waters, the skies, the plants
and the animals will return

I am a witness
I am inspired by the earth's response to her desecration
A tsunami cleanses the earth
a hurricane rearranges rivers
an earthquake is an objection
and we will all have to face ourselves
face our sense of justice
to include all life

We will need to nourish our imagination
to include a new equality
and summon our souls, our hearts and our minds to a justice
which includes all life

"Blind Justice" originally appeared in *Buffalo Shout, Salmon Cry: Conversations on Creation, Land, Justice and Life Together.*

BELOW IS A SONG

Below is a song
It is yours
I glued it to your future
bound familial memories
in its melody

Below is a moment
time
moving breath time
lost time
dead time
present time
future time
any time you want

Below is a clock
keep time
count time
embrace time
make time
make time sweet

Below the clock is a key
Grab the key
find a lock
open it
open your throat
unlock your song

AFTER LISTENING TO
DOUG NEPINAK'S DEATH SONG
For Columpa
July 19, 2005

"I'm singing my death song"
The soft notes of your voice close my ears
open my eyes to blood
I cannot stop seeing your blood

The space between blood cells is awesome,
fluid
Your blood floats old memories,
stills spaces between our visits
My blood stills, barely pumps
in the stillness
memories speak, repeat, rehearse our past

In the melody of your song I hear
this last drama, witness its unfolding

My blood burns heating my body,
compels me to reflect on its journey

Blood cells travel miles
to feed the host
Blood pumps
cleanses flesh, tissue and bone
renewing the body

Soured blood stagnates
Still blood is decadent
Decadent blood insults
assaults the body
disconnects blood
from its origin,
from its sacred trust
renewal, it poisons
Your blood replicates skin cells
in some crazy out of control pattern,
refusing to be tamed
into its original purpose
Out of control this replication
arrests your time with your wife
your children, us…me

Defeated, blood's holy work
feeds this death song
betrays the possibility
"maybe I have one last poem in me"
In its betrayal your blood ignites cells,
inspires them to dance out of control
invades the space between life and death
closes the distance life promised you
I watch your cells skulk about
stealing one more living memory

"Maybe I…"
but there will be no more poems
here in this room of shrinking life

We look at each other
recognize this terrible truth

My blood pumps hope
on ordinary days
I build new memories
My blood hoping ignites,
bloody hope enlightens
My body stretches my time,
moves me to listen to this
your last memory, your last joy
Seeing blood slow awes me,
inspires me and I blush
ashamed, even in your death
you fire up my life

Watching your blood still
bleed hope into mind
I braid this hope
to the undercurrent of despair,
dropping it
one blood drop at a time
into the space between us

This braid is a lifeline
bleeding lust-filled promise
to some incredible
long distance of time

Stubbornly my blood lust for life
pumps desire for one more moment,
one more memory
In its lust my blood
seeks to shrink the space
Desire creates the illusion
of erasing the distance death brings
My blood despairs,
despaired blood shrinks,
transforms, becomes eternity

I remember other dead
bodiless spirits wandering the world
My blood reminds
the distance between the spirit world
and the real world is finite

Blood memory feeds the spirit
re-members the body
re-members eternal joy
re-members endless spider webs of being,
binding me to the dead in a celebration
of where our blood has been

Your blood built memory,
left breath tracks, poems
patterns aimed at arresting death
Blood spent building memory
is the work of artists
Leaving fired Breath Tracks
is the exalted effort of artists
holding space in place,
rendering memory eternal
Poetry cherishes the creation
of joy between the spaces,
the absences and the hard stones
of pathways leading us to one another

My blood resists your departure
My blood is enraged
My blood is a wind
My blood is a hurricane

Your death song is a sweet soft breath,
a poem, a waltz transforming hurricanes
into the wind required to settle my heart
Open my eyes to poetry, to desire,
to the Herculean effort of conjuring
one more poem to rebuild your soul
and halt your early departure

Even as your song ends your life
here in this small room
the raging binds me to future
Its very rampage fires hope,
unleashes floodgates of memories
To review the path we traversed,
quiet memories held captive are freed
They grant me permission
to fill my body with thick blood
ending hopelessness

Even in your death song
your disappearing life
quiets me, humbles me
Your dissipating blood flow
tortures my sense of future,
breaking song into puzzled bits
without rhythm, rhyme or meaning
arresting ties,
those slivers of joy
between long absences
One slim wedge at a time
enlightens and exhilarates
Even now as I say good-bye
you conjure future and I can't weep

On my way out I ask "Why Doug"
Why my friend
Why does Doug have to die of cancer?

The answer floats
in a pool of young blood,
a sewer set apart from the world
leaking our blood
Filled, this unholy cesspool
becomes a pond of decadence
pumping brutality,
tearing at our minds,
renting our souls,
halting the rethreading
of poetry to the need for history
that might sew future
into the tear dresses of tomorrow

Why Doug?

An answer emerges from an Ojibwa elder
firing up the blood I needed to mark my path
to dance across these sharp stones of threat,
the mother country littered my trail with:
"Fish: Someone cast a net and [Doug] got caught."

I came to say good-bye

Sit here next to me, so I can give you a hug

Your thin frail hand taps the bed
Inside I hear my death song
I want to leave with dignity
but I don't say that
I want to extricate my flesh
when my body is done rising,
my heart stops pumping life,
quits purifying my body,
enlivening my soul,
sparking up my next dance
with the same dignity,
but I don't say that

"I love you"
I hold him,
feel the synchronicity of my heartbeat
and his pumping, beating one last beat

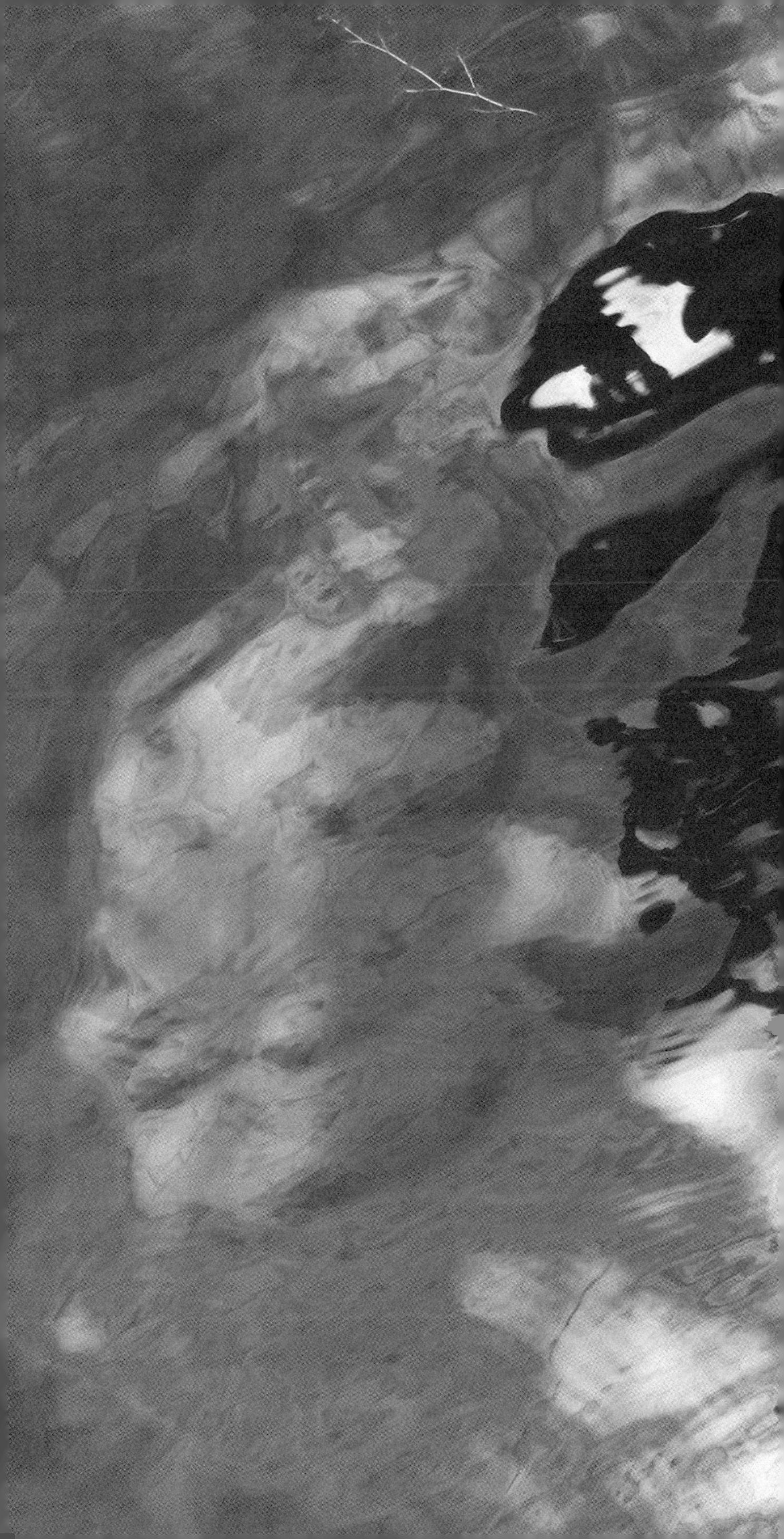

ON WORDS

express, push ᵘᵖ, push o u t
these words fell into me
journeyed through my body
some inspired
others paralyzed

immobilized by words
paralysis creates some kind
of decadent cess pool inside
rendering me a toxic waste
receptacle of cruel language

S

K

Y

WORLD

I dangle at the edge
of this long spiral—Xa'al
From sky world to earth
and back to sky world

SONGLINE OF NIGHT

I enter the fissure inside painted colours
                          of seduction
I want communion with my daughters
                          granddaughters
to approach this dark woman called house
create a sanctuary where dreams are born
encourage them, spirits of fire-flight
cradle us gently, we can be so stupid
not uttering our failings yet holding on
This fissure spawns light, feeds their will
their spirits shine through strands of hair
                          brown glowing red
Cedar cleans the air between skin and sky
I sink under layers of green sea hiding bone splinters
drowned by their own muck teaching us to be careful
breath is braided to cedar's eternal being
                        My spirit circles spaces
conjuring story of how all loves must succeed, then fail
as lovers plummet fathoms to the blackness of the sea
                      stuck between the layers they laugh
Progeny rediscover magic layers they cannot reconcile
Sun's light is swallowed as he rolls over to swing
above sea waves pawing music at the shore
                        We paddle forward
                        She is still roiling
this ocean, moved by her own depth to defy sun's light
It's a deep wave, we so fear depth we are the reason for it
Ocean delivers a slow kiss to earth's waiting hot skin
Sun purses his lips, blushes, steps back and fall is born
                      Sap sleeps under cold's glare
We float to the melody of love sea and sun create

WORDS ARE CRUCIAL

I stop to rest, knees in snow
Gold-laced shallow minds
watch, holler names
squaw, tomahawk chop,
Cleveland Indians
as I rest back bent knees floating
on the white crust below
hot beads of sweat on skin carve
cold sand-paper tracks

words are crucial
words kiss lips
       kill air
       inspire movement
       cross minds
       destroy inertia
elevate or reduce whole standards of normal

snow breathes, buoys my body
       crystallizes thoughts,
tickles the air above my skin
       opens my eyes
diamond-clear thoughts shape behind them
       restoring warmth

BOY IN THE ARCHIVES

I'm here
stashed behind the stacks
of boxes, layers of pipes,
crates of stones,
and masses of flutes
Carefully wrapped
under the blankets
in the damp dark space
where it's often so cold

Over here,
                              here
in the dark shadows
where the light rarely shines,
the sun never visits
and the rain never pierces
Where even song is silent

I can't believe they left me,
they did not come for me
How could they not miss me?
I can't believe my clansmen let them
                    empty me
                    stuff me
                    box me
then lock me up here, in this museum

REMEMBERING MEMORY

These walls hold a voice
words stretched tight
thick with desperation
squeezed from a warrior's truth
hidden beneath a faint peace

Sometimes the voices haunt
the dense air between the walls
The mourner seeks a body
wanders over to mine, enters,
travels the length of me
Cheated of response
the ghosts seek an exit

From the acid scrape
of ghostly desperation
truth leaks through
a parched throat
pulls at the lies
under my skin

Peace, muted by a war cry
whose memories cling
to skin cells unable to escape
from the terrible recall
marking the story

Eyes across the ghostscape
force appropriate courtesy
Lungs conjure manners
from rancid words
boxed to look like gifts

My skin peels off phrases
renouncing aggression,
dirty wars murdering
ancestors, even now can't
stop killing someone else's

COVER UP

Today the sun is brittle
the air crisp, it bites
nips and gnaws at exposed skin
Exposed skin draws glances
up — cover up — hide

How did cover get up from hiding
Hiding seems by nature to be down
down below whomsoever is up
down below whatever defines up

Up — cover up — hide
The sun's light burns crisp
even as the air gnaws and bites
Sunburns birth copper hues
brown skin covers
hides whiteness from skin

How did white skin cover up
Hidden by nature
burnt white it bleeds red
brittle brown, down below
The air crisps — unwelcome

S P I T T I N G

My voice spits red leaves
punctuated dried things
fluttering toward yellow ones
heaping on cold ground

Quiet hurts
compressed leaf words
perforated whispers
under foot—unheard

Golden-hued leaves
fall broken by wind
a caress for someone
consigned to death

People hear voices
soothing golden light
enriching the chatter
and flattering lives

DUCKS

I am leaving this life of fracture,
of compartmentalization and
    broken dreams

My journey began at the edge of the sea,
waves hurling, ducks paddling
    away from buckshot

Barnacled rocks swirl under bare feet,
callouses keeping them safe
    from mutilation

THE EAR OWNS AN ANVIL AND A DRUM

The ear owns an anvil and a
drum
it beats out imaginative rhythms

These tunes move us
to complicate spider's web
simplify the extraordinary
carrying us to coyote

Western palaces of culture
compete with raven
erratic drum beats
Joplin-rock without the roll

disciplines the tip, tip
tippling, swallowing
of amber pints draining
raven of her last squawk

The ear owns an anvil
and a drum

CYBER SPACE

Today cyber space closed the gap between us
like sun fills spaces between green mountains
Each mountain melting a snow-white dress
sliding water into the clefts separating them
plucking dust, twigs, the water sings to us
unsure of whether or not to clutch the hill
or lean in to cleave the birthing river
fill the gorge of this long separation

The dead wood scores the banks, threatens
the edge, the river floods the delta's flat plain
an estuary unfolds at the edge of the inlet
depositing bits to decorate our blank shore
sculptures pleasing those witnesses to birth
of river, spawned by sweet mountain breath

I imagine us together singing a lament
for those who perish in the river's crush
The lament turns into some crazy wish
to sit on dead wood art sculpted by rivers
I cringe along the bank of a different edge
refusing to wade into the bland lake water
It doesn't smell right, the journey upstream
is so absent and you are not there with me
I count on these moments when cyber space
fills me with ocean salt-filled Salish dreams

RAVEN CREATED ROMANCE

I want to see raven,
feel her desire for love
the wind of passion
see her feathers ruffle
watch as she inspires
two sockeye pairs to mate,
leap and play in the sea
study their spawning
imagine their romance
their depth, imagine
unswerving love
consume the experience
taste sockeyes' romance
and feel so overwhelmed
by their surrender
to one night with…

HEDGEBROOK

I'm home again.

Blue-hued dark green islands jut up to reach the sky
still looking as though they want to become flatlands,
valleys and lush green meadows.
They didn't quite make it most of them.
They remain cedar and fir-decked
wedges of earth tied to the deep.

The sea holds these her baby lands,
bathing them in white-capped water
rocking them as though the ferry is still
and the islands moving.
Memory pulls at my skin,
images punch holes in this moment
of awe over the vista the not-quite born islands make.
My body knows these islands.

The story of this corridor belongs to Suquamish boatmen
ferrying families from one end of its territory
to the other. Cedar and ermine skin-clad women ancestors
stand regal in the canoes while brown-skinned men
dip and sing through the slate under-bellied
blue-green water.

Conquest silenced these boatmen
stilling the story of canoes for a time to waken in the first year
of my birth. This meander feels so familiar
I have to wonder whether or not I am impressed.

I'm home again.

This journey from Squamish BC post-cultural prohibition
in 1951 to Hedgebrook in the summer of 2000,
38 years after our emancipation,
is fraught with the urgent watery aloneness
only writers feel.
The aloneness of paddling about in our
various sociological and historical swamps,
weaving snippets of dream word we selected to play with
onto the loom of our imagination
harnessing language
to plough new soil,
create new story,
is thick, omnipresent here.

I'm home again.

My pathway here is strewn with stones,
singing confusing songs of yearning.
My bones, my personal stones,
sing back songs of yearning—
Tsuniquid's yearning.
I watch myself highstep my way to this language
this pen
this paper
this place.

The stones' razored edges bleed white as the faces of my dead
emerge, embossed by the shadows in the centre of each stone.
Between the stones holding their faces, ribbons of light flicker.
Snippets of my busyness shine inside each ribbon of light.
I watch myself steal moments to create art.
Coolly and deliberately I let go of Lucucid
grieve the parking of my original language
and bury it inside my bones.

I pick up the volumes of books cradling the text of this language.
I feel the sand-papering of this language and re-watch as my body
smoothes the rough edges as the words journey through me.
See-yah becomes saskatoon,
si-siutl becomes sea serpent,
Tsuniquid becomes the mother of thought,
thought becomes hidden being,
hidden being becomes a spiral down
to a moment of peace and recognition,
knowing becomes a spiral out to meet the world.
This sea, this new Tsuniquid forms the structure of my being.

I'm home again.

Killer whales sidle their litheness alongside the ferry.
Cedar bows acknowledging my return.
Raven calls out a cackled hello.
Berries look ready to greet me.
Even the sea peels back its tide
to permit a trek across her mud. Just as I land
I can see the wetlands from the hill near my cottage.
The tears come.

I'm home momma.
Haitchka for leading me here.
Haitchka my dead for fussing over language for me.
Haitchka to those who came before me,
for story,
for song,
for dance.
You paved my journey home with light and alacrity.

I am home again.

Suquamish voices are everywhere here.
I am so totally old and so completely new here.
I pull fragments from old file cabinets,
splinters of memory,
bind them together to re-shape my world.
I weave this imagined dream world onto old
Suquamish blankets,
history-hole-punched and worn—
to re-craft today,
to re-member future in this new language.
And I sing I am home again.